CHRISTMAS AT HOME
WITH
Mary & Ma

D0877414

Stirrin' Up Chocolate & Joy

BARBOUR
PUBLISHING

Published by Barbour Publishing, Inc.

ISBN 1-59789-431-1

Recipes were compiled from the following titles, all published by Barbour Publishing, Inc.: *Heart's Delight, Homemade Christmas Cookies, Holiday Desserts, Holiday Jar Mixes, No-Bake Holiday Recipes, Traditional Christmas Favorites, 101 Christmas Recipe Ideas, Holiday Snacks and Appetizers,* and *Homemade Christmas Sweets.*

Cover Design by Greg Jackson, Thinkpen Design, LLC.
Cover and Interior artwork by Karen M. Reilly

Published by Barbour Publishing, Inc., P.O. Box 719, Uhrichsville, Ohio 44683, www.barbourbooks.com

Our mission is to publish and distribute inspirational products offering exceptional value and biblical encouragement to the masses.

Printed in Canada.
5 4 3 2 1

CONTENTS

There are four basic food groups—
milk chocolate, dark chocolate, white chocolate, and chocolate truffles.
UNKNOWN

Meet Mary & Martha. . .

If you love chocolate as much as we do,
then this holiday cookbook is just for you.
Featuring everything from traditional gooey chocolate cookies
to new twists on hot chocolate—if it's chocolate, it's in here!
We'll be appearing throughout the book, offering you tips
and inspiration to make your Christmas just a bit merrier—
and more meaningful.

Ready to stir up some chocolate and joy this season?
Roll up your sleeves, put on that apron, and. . .
Happy cooking!

With love (from our kitchen to yours),
Mary & Martha

Jolly Beverages

There is no beautifier of complexion, or form, or behavior, like the wish to scatter joy.
RALPH WALDO EMERSON

Amaretto Fudge Cappuccino

1 cup boiling water
1 tablespoon instant coffee granules
2 tablespoons amaretto-flavored creamer
1 tablespoon chocolate syrup

Combine water and coffee in mug; stir until coffee is dissolved.
Stir in creamer and chocolate syrup. Serve immediately.

*A good chocolate drink could always use...
more chocolate! Custom-make your
own stirring spoons. Dip a plastic
spoon into melted chocolate.
Allow it to set slightly, resting on
waxed paper, then fill the spoon
bowl with more melted chocolate.
When the chocolate is cooled and
completely set, you can wrap the
spoons in plastic wrap and give them
to other chocolate lovers on your gift list.*

Black Forest Mocha

⅔ cup hot brewed coffee
2 tablespoons chocolate syrup
2 tablespoons light cream
1 tablespoon maraschino cherry juice
Whipped topping

In large mug, stir together coffee, syrup, cream, and cherry juice.
Garnish with whipped topping. Serve immediately.

Caramel Chocolate Cappuccino

1 cup hot water
¾ cup milk
2 tablespoons chocolate syrup
3 tablespoons caramel syrup
1 tablespoon instant coffee granules

Place all ingredients in microwave-safe bowl and microwave on high for
3 minutes or until hot. Stir and pour into mugs. Serve immediately.

Choco Punch

4 (1 ounce) squares semisweet chocolate
½ cup sugar
2 cups hot water
2 quarts milk
1½ teaspoons vanilla
1 quart vanilla ice cream
1 quart club soda
½ pint heavy whipping cream, whipped
Ground cinnamon

In saucepan, combine chocolate and sugar with hot water. Bring to a boil, stirring for approximately 3 minutes. Add milk; continue heating. When hot, beat in vanilla. Remove from heat. Chill; then pour into a punch bowl over ice cream. For sparkle, add club soda. Top with whipped cream and cinnamon.

Choco-Cheesecake Freeze

4 ounces cream cheese, softened
2 cups milk, divided
6 scoops chocolate ice cream

Place cream cheese and 1 cup milk in blender; blend until smooth. Place remaining milk and ice cream in blender and continue to blend until smooth. Serve cold.

Chocolate Eggnog

1 egg
2 teaspoons chocolate syrup
2 teaspoons sugar
2 tablespoons crushed ice
1½ cups milk

Blend all ingredients together. Serve.

Chocolate Hazelnut Coffee

¾ cup hot water
¼ cup hot milk
2 teaspoons hazelnut-flavored instant coffee granules
1 teaspoon cocoa
1 tablespoon dark brown sugar
1 tablespoon whipped topping

Stir together all ingredients. Pour into mugs.
Top with whipped topping and serve immediately.

Got the grumpies this holiday season? As our to-do lists grow beyond our control with shopping, church services, family gatherings, and more. . .it's no wonder! Set aside some quiet time and ask the Lord—our one true Source of joy—to restore the joy of Christmas to your heart.

An angel of the Lord appeared to them, and the glory of the Lord shone around them, and they were terrified. But the angel said to them, "Do not be afraid. I bring you good news of great joy that will be for all the people."
LUKE 2:9–10

Frozen Hot Chocolate

1 cup 2% milk
1 envelope instant hot chocolate mix
2 tablespoons butter
2 ounces milk chocolate, chopped
2 ounces bittersweet chocolate, chopped
6 ice cubes

Heat milk in saucepan over medium-low heat until bubbles just begin to form around edges and mixture is heated through (approximately 2 minutes). Remove from heat; whisk in hot chocolate mix until well blended. Add butter, milk chocolate, and bittersweet chocolate; stir until smooth. Pour chocolate mixture into blender; add ice. Cover; blend on high speed until well blended. Serve immediately.

Malted Milk Ball Chiller

⅓ cup malted milk balls, crushed
1 cup ice cream
1½ tablespoons chocolate syrup
½ cup milk

Place all ingredients in blender and mix until creamy. Serve immediately.

Minty Chocolate Milk

2 tablespoons chocolate syrup
⅛ teaspoon peppermint extract
1 cup milk
1 scoop chocolate ice cream

Stir together chocolate syrup, peppermint flavoring, and milk.
Add ice cream. Serve immediately.

Peanut Butter Hot Chocolate

1 envelope instant hot chocolate mix
2 tablespoons creamy peanut butter

Prepare hot chocolate according to directions on packet. Stir in peanut butter.

Add a little happy to your holiday. When you find yourself feeling overly stressed this Christmas, curl up in your favorite chair with a steaming mug of hot chocolate topped off with loads of whipped topping and read through your favorite portion of scripture. You'll be more joyful for it!

Peppermint Twist
White Hot Chocolate

4 cups milk
3 ounces white chocolate, chopped
⅓ cup red-and-white-striped candy canes or hard peppermint candies, crushed
⅛ teaspoon salt
Whipped topping
Additional red-and-white-striped candy canes, crushed

Bring milk to a simmer in saucepan. Reduce heat to medium-low. Add white chocolate, crushed candy, and salt; whisk until smooth. Ladle into mugs, dividing equally. Serve with whipped topping and additional crushed candy.

Raspberry Truffle Latte

6 ounces hot brewed coffee
2 tablespoons chocolate syrup
2 tablespoons raspberry syrup
½ cup (4 ounces) chocolate ice cream
Whipped topping
Grated chocolate
Fresh raspberries

Mix coffee and flavored syrups in mug. Spoon ice cream into coffee mixture. Add whipped topping, grated chocolate, and fresh raspberries as desired. Makes 1 mug.

Rich Parisian Chocolate

1 cup whole milk
¾ cup heavy cream
¼ cup sugar
5 ounces semisweet chocolate, chopped
Whipped topping

In saucepan over medium-high heat, bring milk, cream, and sugar to a simmer (heating just until bubbles appear around edges of liquid). Remove from heat and add chocolate, stirring until mixture is smooth. If necessary, return pan to low heat while stirring with a wooden spoon until chocolate is melted. Serve in small mugs with whipped topping.

Snowy Cinnamon Cocoa

4 cups milk
1 cup chocolate syrup
1 teaspoon ground cinnamon
Whipped topping
¼ cup semisweet chocolate chips

Place milk and chocolate syrup in microwave-safe bowl and stir. Cook on high for 3 to 4 minutes or until hot. Stir in cinnamon. Pour into four large mugs and garnish with whipped topping and chocolate chips.

Twist of Orange Hot Chocolate

2 cups milk
3 (1 x 2-inch) orange peel strips (orange part only)
⅛ teaspoon ground cinnamon
½ teaspoon instant espresso powder
4 ounces semisweet chocolate, grated

Combine all ingredients in saucepan. Stir over low heat until chocolate melts. Increase heat and bring to a boil, stirring often. Immediately remove from heat and whisk until frothy. Return to heat and bring just to a boil again. Repeat heating and whisking once again. Discard orange peel. Pour hot chocolate into two mugs.

White Chocolate Coffee

3 ounces white chocolate, grated
2 cups whole milk
2 cups hot brewed coffee
Whipped topping (optional)

Place grated white chocolate and milk in microwave-safe bowl and heat for 2 minutes;
stir until mixture is smooth and chocolate is melted completely. Stir in coffee.
Serve in large mugs and garnish with whipped topping.

White Hot Chocolate

3 cups half-and-half, divided
⅔ cup vanilla baking chips
1 cinnamon stick
⅛ teaspoon ground nutmeg
1 teaspoon vanilla
¼ teaspoon almond extract
Ground cinnamon (optional)

Place ¼ cup half-and half, vanilla chips, cinnamon stick, and nutmeg in saucepan; stir over low heat until chips are melted. Discard cinnamon stick. Add remaining half-and-half. Stir until thoroughly heated. Remove from heat, then add vanilla and almond extract. Pour into four mugs. Garnish with cinnamon if desired.

A delectable stirrer for your hot chocolate is a chocolate candy cane. Dip half to three-quarters of the candy cane in melted chocolate and allow it to dry. Enjoy!

World's Best Cocoa

¼ cup cocoa
½ cup sugar
⅓ cup hot water
⅛ teaspoon salt
4 cups milk
¾ teaspoon vanilla

Mix cocoa, sugar, water, and salt in saucepan. Over medium heat, stir constantly until mixture boils. Continue to stir and boil for 1 minute. Add milk and heat. (Do not boil.) Remove from heat and add vanilla; stir well. Pour into four mugs and serve immediately.

Festive Cakes & Pies

Joy delights in joy.
WILLIAM SHAKESPEARE

Black Forest Cake

2 (20 ounce) cans tart pitted cherries, undrained
1 cup sugar
¼ cup cornstarch
1½ teaspoons vanilla
2 (9 inch) chocolate cake layers, baked and cooled
3 cups cold whipping cream
⅓ cup powdered sugar

Drain cherries, reserving ½ cup juice. Combine reserved cherry juice, cherries, sugar, and cornstarch in saucepan. Cook and stir over low heat until thickened. Add vanilla; stir then set aside. Divide each cake layer in half horizontally. Crumble one of the half layers; set aside. Beat cold whipping cream and powdered sugar in large bowl with electric mixer on high speed until stiff peaks form. Reserve 1½ cups whipped cream for decorative piping. Place one cake layer on a serving plate. Spread with 1 cup whipped cream; top with ¾ cup cherry topping. Top with second cake layer, 1 cup whipped cream, and ¾ cup cherry topping; top with third cake layer. Frost cake sides with remaining whipped cream; pat gently with reserved cake crumbs. Spoon reserved 1½ cups whipped cream into pastry bag fitted with star tip; pipe around top and bottom edges of cake. Spoon remaining topping over top of cake.

Black Forest Cream Pie

CRUST:
1 (15 ounce) package all-ready piecrusts

Using 9-inch pie pan with removable bottom, prepare one crust according to package directions. Bake at 450° until lightly browned, 9 to 11 minutes. Allow to cool completely. (Leftover crust may be refrigerated for later use.)

FILLING:
6 ounces semisweet baking chocolate, chopped
2 tablespoons margarine
¼ cup powdered sugar

1 (8 ounce) package cream cheese, softened
1 cup cherry pie filling

While crust is cooling, melt chocolate and margarine over low heat, stirring continually. When melted, remove from heat. In bowl, beat together powdered sugar and cream cheese until smooth. Stir in chocolate mixture; beat until smooth. Fold in pie filling. Spread mixture evenly in prepared pie shell. Chill for 1 hour.

(cont.)

TOPPING:
1 cup whipping cream, whipped
1 ounce semisweet baking chocolate, grated
1⅓ cups cherry pie filling
Chocolate curls (optional)

In separate bowl, combine whipped cream and grated chocolate. Spread evenly over cooled chocolate layer. Spread pie filling around outer edge of pie. Refrigerate until ready to serve. If desired, garnish with chocolate curls.

Chocolate Almond Pie

½ cup milk
16 large marshmallows
6 chocolate-almond candy bars
1 cup whipping cream, whipped
1 (9 inch) piecrust, baked and cooled
Sweetened whipped cream
Chocolate curls

Heat milk in saucepan until hot; dissolve marshmallows in hot milk.
Break and add candy bars. Stir until melted. Remove from heat and cool.
Fold in 1 cup whipped cream. Pour into baked 9-inch piecrust.
Refrigerate until set. Serve with sweetened whipped cream and chocolate curls.

Chocolate…
More chocolate…
A little more chocolate…
Life is good!

Chocolate Caramel Cake

1⅔ cups flour
1½ cups sugar
⅔ cup cocoa
1½ teaspoons baking powder
1 teaspoon salt
1½ cups buttermilk

½ cup shortening
2 eggs
1½ teaspoons vanilla
30 caramels
1 (14 ounce) can sweetened
  condensed milk

Beat first nine ingredients in large mixing bowl on low speed, scraping sides of bowl, until blended. Beat on high, scraping sides occasionally, for an additional 3 minutes. Pour half of cake batter into greased and floured 9 x 13-inch baking pan; bake at 350° for 15 minutes. In the meantime, melt caramels and sweetened condensed milk together. Spread over warm cake. Spread remaining cake batter on top of caramel mixture. Bake for an additional 15 minutes or until done. Serve warm with vanilla ice cream for a tasty treat.

Chocolate Cheesecake

½ cup butter or margarine, melted
1½ cups graham cracker crumbs
½ cup sugar
⅔ cup water
1 envelope gelatin, unflavored
2 (8 ounce) packages cream cheese, softened

4 (1 ounce) squares semisweet chocolate, melted
1 (14 ounce) can sweetened condensed milk
1 teaspoon vanilla
1 cup frozen whipped topping, thawed

In 9-inch springform pan, mix together butter, graham cracker crumbs, and sugar. Press firmly on bottom of pan (do not line sides). Pour water into small saucepan. Sprinkle gelatin over water and let stand for 1 minute. Over low heat, stir until gelatin dissolves; set aside. In large bowl, beat cream cheese and chocolate until fluffy. Gradually beat in sweetened condensed milk. Add vanilla and beat until smooth. Stir gelatin mixture into cream cheese mixture. Fold in whipped topping. Pour mixture into prepared pan. Chill in refrigerator for 3 hours or until set. Garnish with whipped topping. Keep refrigerated.

Chocolate Chiffon Cake

2 cups hot water
⅔ cup cocoa
2 cups flour
4 teaspoons baking powder
½ teaspoon baking soda
1 teaspoon salt

2 cups sugar
½ cup vegetable oil
1 teaspoon vanilla
6 eggs, separated
½ teaspoon cream of tartar

Combine hot water and cocoa. Boil for 1 minute. Cool. In separate bowl, sift flour, baking powder, baking soda, salt, and sugar. Add cooled cocoa syrup, vegetable oil, vanilla, and egg yolks. Blend until smooth. Beat egg whites and cream of tartar until very stiff. Carefully fold egg whites into first mixture. Bake in ungreased tube pan at 350° for approximately 50 minutes.

COCOA FROSTING:

1½ cups cold milk
1 envelope whipped topping mix
1 (4-serving size) package chocolate fudge instant pudding

Pour cold milk in mixing bowl; add contents of whipped topping envelope and pudding mix. Beat on low for 1 minute. Slowly increase speed and beat for 4 to 6 minutes.

Chocolate Chip Cheesecake

1½ cups chocolate sandwich cookie crumbs
3 tablespoons butter, melted
3 (3 ounce) packages cream cheese, softened
1 (14 ounce) can sweetened condensed milk
2 teaspoons vanilla
3 eggs
1 cup semisweet chocolate chips, divided
1 teaspoon flour

Combine cookie crumbs and butter; press into 9-inch springform pan. Beat cream cheese until fluffy, then beat in milk, vanilla, and eggs. Toss ½ cup chocolate chips with flour to coat; stir into cream cheese mixture. Pour into prepared pan and sprinkle with remaining chips. Bake at 300° for 1 hour or until cake springs back when lightly touched. Cool. Chill. Serve.

Chocolate Chip Rocky Road Pie

½ cup butter
1 cup dark brown sugar, packed
1 egg, slightly beaten
2 tablespoons hot water
1 teaspoon vanilla
1 cup flour, sifted
½ teaspoon baking powder

¼ teaspoon salt
⅛ teaspoon baking soda
½ cup nuts, chopped
1 cup mini semisweet chocolate chips, divided
1 cup miniature marshmallows, divided

Melt butter over low heat; mix in brown sugar until well blended. Add egg, hot water, and vanilla. In separate bowl, stir together flour, baking powder, salt, and baking soda. Add to sugar mixture; mix well. Mix in nuts, half of chocolate chips, and half of marshmallows. Spread mixture into two 9-inch pie plates; sprinkle with remaining chips and marshmallows. Bake at 350° for 20 minutes. Cool.

Chocolate Fudge Upside-Down Cake

2 tablespoons shortening
1 cup milk
1 teaspoon salt
2 teaspoons baking powder

1½ cups sugar
2 cups flour
1 teaspoon vanilla
3 tablespoons cocoa

Mix together all cake batter ingredients and spread in 9 x 13-inch baking pan;
sprinkle with nuts if desired. Set aside.

TOPPING:
2 cups sugar
½ cup cocoa
2½ cups boiling water

Mix sugar with cocoa and spread over batter in pan. Then pour boiling water over top.
Bake at 375° for 30 minutes.

Chocolate Peanut Butter Pie

2 cups extra crunchy peanut butter
1 (8 ounce) package fat-free cream cheese, softened
2 cups powdered sugar
1 cup skim milk
3 (8 ounce) containers frozen whipped topping, thawed
3 (9 inch) prepared chocolate crumb piecrusts

Mix peanut butter and cream cheese until smooth. Add powdered sugar, milk, and 12 ounces (1½ containers) whipped topping. Blend thoroughly and pour into piecrusts, spreading evenly. Top each pie with 4 ounces whipped topping. (These pies freeze and keep well.) For added freshness, store pies in 1-gallon freezer bags.

Chocolate Pecan Pie

2 (1 ounce) squares unsweetened chocolate
2 tablespoons butter
3 eggs
½ cup sugar
¾ cup dark corn syrup
1 cup pecans, halved
1 (9 inch) piecrust, unbaked

Melt chocolate and butter together. Beat together eggs, sugar, chocolate mixture, and corn syrup. Mix in pecans. Pour into piecrust. Bake at 375° for 40 to 50 minutes, just until set. Serve slightly warm or cold with ice cream or whipped topping.

Chocolate Pie

3 (1 ounce) squares semisweet
   chocolate
1 (14 ounce) can sweetened
   condensed milk
¼ teaspoon salt
¼ cup hot water

2 egg yolks
1 teaspoon vanilla
1 cup frozen whipped topping,
   thawed
1 (9 inch) prepared piecrust
Additional whipped topping
Chocolate shavings

In large saucepan, combine chocolate, sweetened condensed milk, and salt. Cook over medium heat until thick and bubbly, stirring constantly. Add water and egg yolks, stirring quickly until mixture is thick and bubbly again. Remove from heat and stir in vanilla. Allow to cool for 15 minutes. Chill in refrigerator for an additional 20 to 30 minutes; stir. Fold whipped topping into cooled chocolate mixture; stir. Pour chocolate mixture into prepared piecrust. Chill for 2½ to 3 hours or until chocolate is set. Cover with additional whipped topping. Garnish with chocolate shavings. Keep refrigerated.

Chocolate Ripple Orange Cake

CAKE MIXTURE:

1 cup butter or margarine,
   softened
1 cup sugar
3 large eggs
1 cup sour cream

1¾ cups flour
1 teaspoon baking powder
1 teaspoon baking soda
Zest of 1 orange

Cream butter and sugar until light and fluffy. Add eggs; beat for 1 minute at low speed. Blend in sour cream. Add dry ingredients and zest; blend thoroughly. Spoon one-fourth of cake batter into greased and floured 10-inch tube pan. Alternate layers of cake mixture with filling, finishing with final layer of cake mixture. Bake at 325° for 60 minutes. Cool for 10 minutes and invert. When cake is completely cooled, drizzle with topping.

FILLING:

½ cup sugar
1 heaping tablespoon cocoa

3 tablespoons ground cinnamon

In small bowl, mix sugar, cocoa, and cinnamon.

(cont.)

TOPPING:
¼ cup orange juice
⅓ cup powdered sugar

While cake is cooling, mix juice and powdered sugar.
Boil for a few minutes, then drizzle over cake.

Chocolate Turtle Cheesecake

1 (7 ounce) package caramels
¼ cup evaporated milk
½ cup pecans, chopped
1 (9 inch) prepared chocolate crumb piecrust
2 (3 ounce) packages cream cheese, softened
½ cup sour cream
1¼ cups milk
1 (3.9 ounce) package chocolate instant pudding
½ cup fudge topping
¼ cup pecans, chopped

Place caramels and evaporated milk in large saucepan. Heat over medium heat, stirring constantly until smooth. Stir in ½ cup pecans. Pour into piecrust. Combine cream cheese, sour cream, milk, and pudding mix in blender. Process until smooth. Pour pudding mixture over caramel layer, covering evenly. Loosely cover pie and chill until set. Drizzle fudge topping over pudding layer in decorative pattern. Sprinkle with ¼ cup pecans. Cover and loosely chill in refrigerator.

Cookies and Cream Pie

1 (3.9 ounce) package chocolate instant pudding
1 (8 ounce) container frozen whipped topping, thawed
1½ cups chocolate sandwich cookie crumbs
1 (9 inch) prepared chocolate crumb piecrust

Prepare pudding according to pie filling directions on package; allow to set. When pudding is ready, fold in whipped topping. Add cookie crumbs; stir. Pour mixture into prepared piecrust. Freeze pie until firm. Thaw in refrigerator before serving.

Dirt Cake

1 (16 ounce) package chocolate sandwich cookies
1 (8 ounce) package cream cheese, softened
½ cup (1 stick) butter, softened
1 cup powdered sugar
1 (8 ounce) container frozen whipped topping, thawed
2 (3 ounce) packages vanilla instant pudding
3 cups milk
1 teaspoon vanilla

Crush cookies and put half of crumbs in 9 x 13-inch baking pan. Mix cream cheese and butter until smooth. Mix in powdered sugar. Fold in whipped topping. In separate bowl, mix pudding mixes, milk, and vanilla. Fold in cream cheese mixture. Stir well. Pour batter on top of crumbs. Sprinkle remaining crumbs on top. Refrigerate.

Earthquake Cake

1 cup nuts, chopped
1 cup flaked coconut, finely chopped
1 German chocolate cake mix
1 (8 ounce) package cream cheese, softened
1 cup shortening
1 pound powdered sugar

Grease 9 x 13-inch baking pan; put nuts and coconut in pan. Prepare cake mix according to package directions and spread on top of nuts and coconut. Then beat together cream cheese, shortening, and powdered sugar until fluffy. Drop by spoonfuls on top of cake batter in pan. Bake at 350° for 40 minutes or until done when tested.

Fudge Ribbon Cake

CHEESE MIXTURE:

2 tablespoons butter, softened
1 (8 ounce) package cream
  cheese, softened
¼ cup sugar
1 tablespoon cornstarch

1 egg
2 tablespoons sugar
1 egg
2 tablespoons milk
½ teaspoon vanilla

Cream 2 tablespoons butter with cream cheese; add ¼ cup sugar and cornstarch.
Add 1 egg and 2 tablespoons sugar. Then add 1 egg, milk, and vanilla.
Beat at high speed until smooth and creamy. Set aside.

CAKE MIXTURE:

2 cups flour
2 cups sugar
1 teaspoon salt
1 teaspoon baking powder
½ teaspoon baking soda
½ cup butter, softened

1 cup milk
⅓ cup milk
2 eggs
3 squares unsweetened
  chocolate, melted
1 teaspoon vanilla

(cont.)

Grease and flour bottom of 9 x 13-inch baking pan. Combine flour with sugar, salt, baking powder, and baking soda in large mixing bowl. Add butter and 1 cup milk. Blend well at low speed. Add ⅓ cup milk, eggs, chocolate, and vanilla; continue beating 1½ minutes at low speed. Spread half of batter in pan. Spoon cheese mixture over batter. Top with remaining batter. Bake at 350° for 50 to 60 minutes. Cool and frost if desired.

Italian Love Cake

1 chocolate cake mix
2 (16 ounce) containers ricotta cheese
4 eggs
1 teaspoon vanilla
¾ cup sugar
1 (5.9 ounce) package chocolate instant pudding
1 cup milk
1 (8 ounce) container frozen whipped topping, thawed

Prepare cake mix according to package directions. Pour batter into greased and floured
9 x 13-inch baking pan. In a separate bowl, combine ricotta cheese, eggs, vanilla,
and sugar. Mix well and spoon over top of cake batter. Bake at 350° for 1 hour.
Cake will rise to the top. Cool. Mix pudding with milk; fold in whipped topping.
Spread over cooled cake and refrigerate.

Mississippi Mud Cake

CAKE:
2 cups sugar
1 cup shortening
4 eggs
1½ cups flour
¼ teaspoon salt
⅓ cup cocoa
1 cup pecans, chopped
3 teaspoons vanilla
7 ounces marshmallow creme

Cream sugar and shortening. Add eggs one at a time, stirring after each addition. Sift together flour, salt, and cocoa; add to creamed mixture. Stir in nuts and vanilla. Pour into 9 x 13-inch baking pan. Bake at 350° for 30 minutes. Top with marshmallow creme as soon as cake comes out of oven. Cool before frosting.

(cont.)

FROSTING:
1 cup (2 sticks) margarine, softened
⅓ cup cocoa
1 box powdered sugar
1 teaspoon vanilla
½ cup pecans, chopped
¼ cup canned milk

Mix all ingredients, then frost cake. Keep cake refrigerated.

Oatmeal Chocolate Chip Cake

1¾ cups boiling water
1 cup oats
1 cup brown sugar
1 cup sugar
½ cup margarine
2 large eggs
1¾ cups flour

1 teaspoon baking soda
½ teaspoon salt
1 tablespoon cocoa
1 cup semisweet chocolate chips,
    divided
¾ cup walnuts, chopped

Preheat oven to 350°. Pour boiling water over oats; let stand at room temperature for 10 minutes. Add sugars and margarine to oatmeal. Stir until margarine melts. Add eggs and mix well. Then add flour, baking soda, salt, and cocoa, stirring until well blended. Add half of chocolate chips. Pour batter into greased 9 x 13-inch baking pan. Sprinkle nuts and remaining chocolate chips on top. Bake for 40 minutes.

Choose someone in need of a little encouragement this holiday. Send her a card (sign it anonymously)...and write a heartfelt note about her importance and contribution to the world. Thank her for being her special self! To make it doubly appreciated, include a plate of something scrumptious and chocolaty.

Snickerdoodle Cake

1 German chocolate cake mix
1 (14 ounce) package caramels
½ cup margarine
⅓ cup milk
¾ cup semisweet chocolate chips
1 cup walnuts, chopped

Prepare cake mix according to package directions. Pour half of batter into greased 9 x 13-inch baking pan. Bake at 350° for 20 minutes. Melt caramels with margarine and milk in saucepan over low heat, stirring frequently. Pour over baked cake. Sprinkle with chocolate chips and nuts. Spoon remaining cake batter over caramel layer. Bake at 250° for 20 minutes. Increase temperature to 350° and bake for an additional 10 minutes.

Sour Cream Chocolate Chip Cake

6 tablespoons butter, softened
1 cup sugar
2 eggs
1⅓ cups flour
1½ teaspoons baking powder
1 teaspoon baking soda
1 teaspoon ground cinnamon
1 cup sour cream
1 cup (6 ounces) mini semisweet chocolate chips
1 tablespoon sugar

Mix butter and 1 cup sugar until blended. Beat in eggs one at a time. In separate bowl, stir baking powder, baking soda, and cinnamon into flour, then blend with creamed mixture. Mix in sour cream. Pour batter into greased and floured 8 x 10-inch baking pan. Scatter chocolate chips evenly over batter. Then sprinkle 1 tablespoon sugar over top. Bake at 350° for 35 minutes or until cake just begins to pull away from sides of pan.

Christmassy Candies

A joy that's shared is a joy made double.
ENGLISH PROVERB

Cheery Cherry Christmas Fudge

1 (8 ounce) can almond paste
1 (14 ounce) can sweetened condensed milk, divided
Red food coloring
1¾ cups semisweet chocolate chips
Red candied-cherry halves
Almonds, sliced

Line 8 x 8-inch baking pan with aluminum foil, extending foil over edges of pan. Beat almond paste and ¼ cup sweetened condensed milk in small bowl until well mixed. Add food coloring and beat until blended. Refrigerate for about 1 hour or until firm. Spread onto bottom of prepared pan. Place chocolate chips and remaining sweetened condensed milk in medium microwave-safe bowl. Microwave on high for 1 to 1½ minutes or until chocolate is melted and smooth. Spread over top of almond paste layer. Cover and refrigerate until firm. Use edges of foil to lift fudge out of pan. Peel off foil and cut fudge into squares. Garnish with cherry halves and almonds. Store in airtight container in refrigerator.

Fill old-fashioned glass canning jars with homemade treats like spiced hot chocolate mix, bean soup mix, or a cookie mix. Dress it up with a circle of holiday fabric to fit under the jar ring.

Choco-Butterscotch Crisps

1 cup butterscotch chips
½ cup peanut butter
4 cups crispy rice cereal
1 cup semisweet chocolate chips
2 tablespoons butter
1 tablespoon water
½ cup powdered sugar

Melt butterscotch chips and peanut butter over very low heat, stirring occasionally.
Add cereal and mix well. Press half of mixture in 8 x 8-inch greased baking pan and chill.
Melt chocolate chips, butter, and water in top of double boiler and add powdered sugar.
Spread over chilled mixture and press in remainder of cereal mixture. Cut and chill.

Chocolate-Covered Cherries

2½ cups sugar
¼ cup margarine
1 tablespoon milk
½ teaspoon almond extract
4 (4 ounce) jars maraschino cherries with stems, drained
2 cups semisweet chocolate chips
2 tablespoons shortening

In medium bowl, combine sugar, margarine, milk, and almond extract; stir. On lightly floured surface, knead mixture into large ball. Roll into 1-inch balls. Flatten balls into 2-inch circles. Leaving stems sticking out, wrap cherries in circles by lightly rolling in hands. Place wrapped cherries on sheet of waxed paper and chill in refrigerator for at least 4 hours. In medium saucepan over medium heat, melt chocolate chips and shortening. Holding balls by stems of cherries sticking out, dip chilled balls into chocolate mixture. Chill in refrigerator.

Chocolate-Drizzled
Peanut Butter Fudge

1½ cups sugar
1 cup (5 ounces) evaporated milk
¼ cup butter
1 jar marshmallow creme
1 cup crunchy peanut butter
1 teaspoon vanilla
2 (1 ounce) squares semisweet chocolate

Grease 8 x 8- or 9 x 9-inch baking pan. Combine sugar, milk, and butter in microwave-safe bowl. Microwave on high for 6 minutes, stirring halfway through. Cook 4 to 6 minutes more or until small amount of sugar forms soft ball when dropped in water or until temperature reaches 236°. Add remaining ingredients, except chocolate. Beat until well blended. Pour into pan. Cool for 30 minutes. Melt chocolate for 1 to 2 minutes. Stir after 30 seconds. Drizzle over top of fudge.

Chocolate Peanut Clusters

2 tablespoons creamy peanut butter
1 cup semisweet chocolate chips
1 cup butterscotch chips
2 cups salted peanuts

In medium saucepan, combine peanut butter and chocolate and butterscotch chips.
Cook over medium heat until chips are melted and smooth. Remove from heat
and add peanuts. Drop by rounded spoonfuls onto waxed paper.

Chocolate Peppermint Pretzels

PRETZEL DOUGH:
1 cup powdered sugar
½ cup butter, softened
½ cup shortening
1 egg
1½ teaspoons vanilla
2½ cups flour
½ cup cocoa
1 teaspoon salt
¼ cup peppermint candy canes, crushed

Mix sugar, butter, shortening, egg, and vanilla. Stir in dry ingredients, except candy canes. Knead level tablespoons of dough by hand until dough reaches right consistency for molding. Roll into pencil-like ropes approximately 9 inches long. Twist into pretzel shapes on ungreased baking sheet. Bake at 375° until set, about 9 minutes. Let stand for 1 to 2 minutes before removing from baking sheet; cool completely. Dip tops of pretzels into coating and sprinkle with crushed candy canes. *(cont.)*

CHOCOLATE COATING:
2 (1 ounce) squares unsweetened chocolate
2 tablespoons butter
2 cups powdered sugar
3–4 tablespoons water

Melt chocolate and butter; remove from heat. Beat in sugar and water until smooth.

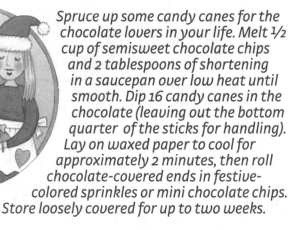

Spruce up some candy canes for the chocolate lovers in your life. Melt ½ cup of semisweet chocolate chips and 2 tablespoons of shortening in a saucepan over low heat until smooth. Dip 16 candy canes in the chocolate (leaving out the bottom quarter of the sticks for handling). Lay on waxed paper to cool for approximately 2 minutes, then roll chocolate-covered ends in festive-colored sprinkles or mini chocolate chips. Store loosely covered for up to two weeks.

Chocolate Snowballs

1¼ cups butter, softened
⅔ cup sugar
1 teaspoon vanilla
2 cups flour
⅛ teaspoon salt
½ cup cocoa
2 cups pecans, chopped
½ cup powdered sugar

In medium bowl, cream butter and sugar until light and fluffy. Stir in vanilla. Sift together flour, salt, and cocoa; stir into creamed mixture. Mix in pecans until well blended. Cover and chill for at least 2 hours. Preheat oven to 350°. Roll chilled dough into 1-inch balls. Place about 2 inches apart on ungreased cookie sheets. Bake for 20 minutes in preheated oven. Roll in powdered sugar when cooled.

Chocolate Truffles

6 (1 ounce) squares dark semisweet chocolate
3 tablespoons unsalted butter
2 tablespoons powdered sugar
3 egg yolks
1 tablespoon rum flavoring
½ cup semisweet chocolate, finely grated

Melt chocolate in top of double boiler over boiling water. Blend in butter and sugar, stirring until sugar dissolves. Remove from heat and add egg yolks one at a time, beating well after each addition. Stir in rum flavoring. Place in bowl covered with waxed paper overnight, but do not chill. Shape into 1-inch balls and roll in grated chocolate. Best served after a day or two.

Cookie Bark

1 (20 ounce) package chocolate sandwich cookies
2 (18½ ounce) packages white chocolate

Line 10 x 15-inch jellyroll pan with waxed paper. Coat paper with nonstick cooking spray; set aside. Break half of cookies into coarse pieces and place in large bowl. In microwave-safe bowl, melt one package of white chocolate in microwave. Quickly fold melted chocolate into broken cookie pieces. Pour mixture into prepared pan and spread to cover half of pan. Repeat process with remaining chocolate and cookies. Refrigerate until solid. Remove from pan and carefully peel off waxed paper. Place bark on large cutting board and cut into pieces with a large knife. Store in airtight container.

Share your culinary talents with the chocolate lovers in your life—and give the gift of delicious confections from your kitchen. Place a variety of chocolate delights in a holiday tin and attach a handwritten note with love.

Fantastic Fudge

⅔ cup evaporated milk
1⅔ cups sugar
1½ cups chocolate chips
1½ cups miniature marshmallows
½ teaspoon salt
1 teaspoon vanilla

In saucepan, combine milk and sugar; bring to a boil and continue boiling for 5 minutes. Add chocolate chips and marshmallows. Stir until blended. Add salt and vanilla and pour into greased 9 x 9-inch baking dish to cool.

FLAVOR VARIATIONS:

MOCHA:
Dissolve 2 teaspoons instant coffee granules in 1 teaspoon hot water. Add with chocolate.
(cont.)

Mint:
Substitute ¾ cup mint chips and ¾ cup chocolate chips for 1½ cups chocolate chips.

Marble:
Substitute white chocolate chips for chocolate chips. After pouring fudge mixture into baking dish, drizzle with melted chocolate chips and swirl with knife for marble effect.

Chocolate Orange:
Add 2 teaspoons orange zest.

Peanut Butter:
Substitute peanut butter chips for chocolate chips.

White Almond:
Substitute white chocolate chips and ½ cup slivered almonds for chocolate chips.

Maple:
Substitute butterscotch chips and add maple flavoring to taste.

Mocha Fudge

1 cup pecans, chopped
3 cups semisweet chocolate chips
1 (14 ounce) can sweetened condensed milk
2 tablespoons strong brewed coffee, room temperature
1 teaspoon ground cinnamon
⅛ teaspoon salt
1 teaspoon vanilla

Line 8 x 8-inch baking pan with aluminum foil. Butter foil and set pan aside. Microwave pecans on high for 4 minutes, being sure to stir after each minute. In 2-quart microwave-safe bowl, mix chocolate chips, milk, coffee, cinnamon, and salt. Microwave on high for 1½ minutes. Stir until smooth. Add pecans and vanilla to chocolate mixture and stir thoroughly. Cover and refrigerate until firm, about 2 hours. Remove from pan and cut into squares of desired size.

No-Bake Christmas Graham Fudge

2 cups semisweet chocolate chips
¼ cup butter or margarine
2½ cups graham cracker crumbs
1½ cups almonds or pecans, chopped
1 (14 ounce) can sweetened condensed milk
1 teaspoon vanilla

Melt chocolate chips and butter together until smooth. In large bowl, combine graham cracker crumbs and nuts. Stir in sweetened condensed milk and vanilla until crumbs are moistened, then stir in chocolate mixture until mixed. Pat evenly into greased 9 x 13-inch baking pan. Let stand at room temperature for 2 hours before cutting into squares.

Chocolate and coffee go well together. Create a welcoming atmosphere in your home by placing an aromatic candle—vanilla is my favorite—in a bowl or jar. Fill the space around the candle with whole coffee beans up to an inch from the top of the candle. Then drink coffee and eat chocolate by candlelight.

Ohio Buckeyes

1 cup margarine, melted
2 cups peanut butter
4 cups powdered sugar
1 teaspoon vanilla
1 (2 x 2 inch) piece of paraffin
3 cups semisweet chocolate chips

Cream together maragarine, peanut butter, powdered sugar, and vanilla. Chill in refrigerator for a few hours, then roll into balls approximately ¾ inch in diameter. Chill balls in refrigerator for at least 8 hours. Melt paraffin and chocolate in double boiler. Using toothpick, dip each ball into chocolate mixture, twirling off excess chocolate. Place on waxed paper to set up.

Quick Chocolate Drops

3 cups quick-cooking oats
1 cup flaked coconut
6 tablespoons cocoa
½ cup butter
½ cup milk
2 cups sugar
½ teaspoon vanilla

Mix oats, coconut, and cocoa. In saucepan, combine butter, milk, sugar, and vanilla; heat until almost boiling (but do not boil). Pour over dry mixture and stir well. Drop by spoonfuls onto buttered waxed paper. Chill until firm.

Quick Chocolate Truffles

3⅓ to 4 cups (20 to 24 ounces) milk chocolate chips
1 (8 ounce) container frozen whipped topping, thawed
1¼ cups graham cracker crumbs

Microwave chocolate chips on medium-high heat for 1 minute. Stir; microwave 10 to 20 seconds longer or until chips are melted. Stir occasionally during melting process. Cool for about 30 minutes, stirring occasionally. Fold in whipped topping. Drop by rounded teaspoonfuls onto waxed paper–lined cookie sheets. Freeze until firm, about 1½ hours. Shape into balls and roll in graham cracker crumbs. Refrigerate in airtight containers. If desired, truffles may be frozen and then removed from freezer 30 minutes before serving.

Rocky Road Candy

2 cups (1 bag) semisweet chocolate chips
½ bag colored miniature marshmallows
⅓ cup pecans, chopped

Melt chocolate over low heat, or use double boiler or microwave.
Stir in marshmallows and pecans. Spoon onto waxed paper. Form into log.
Refrigerate for 2 hours. Slice into ½-inch pieces.

A great gift for a chocolate lover is a basket filled with chocolaty treats, such as a variety of candy bars, brownies with fudge icing, truffles, a German chocolate cake mix, fudge, chocolate syrup, an instant chocolate pudding mix, chocolate-covered pretzels, a hot cocoa mix. . .
The possibilities are endless!

White Chocolate-Covered Pretzels

6 (1 ounce) squares white chocolate
1 (15 ounce) package mini twist pretzels
¼ cup red and green candy sprinkles (optional)

Melt white chocolate in top of double boiler, stirring constantly. Dip pretzel halfway into white chocolate, completely covering half of pretzel. Roll in topping if desired and lay on waxed paper. Continue process until no white chocolate remains. Place pretzels in refrigerator for 15 minutes to harden. Store in airtight container.

Give an anonymous gift of homemade chocolate candies to a person in need of a little pick-me-up during the holiday season. You'll be amazed at what a little kindness can do.

Holiday Cookies & Bars

A joyful heart is the inevitable result of a heart burning with love.
MOTHER TERESA

Big Chocolate Chip Cookies

1 cup margarine
1 cup brown sugar
1 egg
1 teaspoon vanilla
2 cups flour
1 teaspoon baking soda
½ teaspoon salt
1 cup rolled oats
2 cups chocolate chips
½ cup nuts (optional)
½ cup raisins (optional)

Combine margarine, brown sugar, egg, and vanilla. Add flour, baking soda, and salt. Add oats, chocolate chips, and, if desired, nuts and raisins; mix well. Measure ¼ cup dough for each cookie, making each cookie 3 inches in diameter and ½ inch thick. Bake on lightly greased cookie sheets for 15 minutes. Let cool for 5 minutes before removing from sheets.

To help your chocolate chips maintain their shape in your desserts, freeze the chocolate chips before adding them to your ready-to-bake cookie dough or cake batter.

Brownie Christmas Trees

BROWNIE LAYER:

1 (19.8 to 21.5 ounce) plain brownie mix
½ cup butter or margarine, melted

Prepare brownie mix according to package directions, except substitute melted butter for oil. Pour batter into 9 x13-inch baking pan lined with greased foil.
Bake at 350° for 30 to 33 minutes. Cool.

FROSTING:

3 cups powdered sugar
½ cup butter or margarine, softened
1 teaspoon vanilla
3 to 4 tablespoons milk

3 to 4 drops green food coloring
2 to 3 tablespoons miniature candy-coated chocolate pieces
28 (1 to 1½ inch) pretzel rod pieces

Combine powdered sugar, butter, vanilla, and enough milk for desired consistency. Add food coloring. Remove brownie from pan and remove foil. When completely cool, frost. Cut brownie into four (3 inch) rows. Cut each row into seven triangles. Press chocolate pieces into frosting. Insert pretzel into one side for tree trunk. Makes 28 trees.

Caramel Brownies

2 cups sugar
¾ cup cocoa
1 cup vegetable oil
4 eggs
¼ cup milk
1½ cups flour
1 teaspoon salt

1 teaspoon baking powder
1 cup semisweet chocolate
  chips
1 cup walnuts, chopped, divided
1 (14 ounce) package caramels
1 (14 ounce) can sweetened
  condensed milk

In mixing bowl, combine sugar, cocoa, oil, eggs, and milk. Combine flour, salt, and baking powder; add to egg mixture and mix well. Fold in chocolate chips and ½ cup walnuts. Spoon two-thirds of batter into greased 9 x 13-inch baking pan. Bake at 350° for 12 minutes. Meanwhile, in saucepan, heat caramels and condensed milk over low heat until caramels are melted. Pour over baked brownie layer. Sprinkle with remaining walnuts. Drop remaining batter by teaspoonfuls over caramel layer; carefully swirl brownie batter with a knife. Bake 35 to 40 minutes longer or until toothpick inserted near center comes out with moist crumbs. Cool on wire rack.

Chewy Chocolate Bars

2 cups semisweet chocolate chips
1 (14 ounce) can sweetened condensed milk
¾ cup butter, softened
1¼ cups brown sugar, packed
2 eggs
1½ cups flour
¾ cup rolled oats
½ teaspoon salt

Melt chocolate chips with milk; set aside. Cream butter and brown sugar until soft; beat in eggs. Blend flour, rolled oats, and salt into creamed mixture. Spread half of batter into greased 9 x 13-inch baking pan. Spread chocolate mixture on top of batter. Spread remaining batter over chocolate layer. Bake at 350° for 35 minutes. Cool and cut into bars.

Chewy Chocolate Cookies

COOKIES:

½ cup shortening
1 cup sugar
1 large egg
1 teaspoon vanilla
1¾ cups flour
½ teaspoon baking soda

¼ teaspoon salt
½ cup cocoa
½ cup milk
½ cup pecans, chopped
24 large marshmallows, cut in half
Pecans, halved

Beat shortening on medium speed. Gradually add sugar. Beat well. Add egg and vanilla and beat well. In separate bowl, combine flour, baking soda, salt, and cocoa. Slowly add to shortening mixture alternately with milk. When alternating, begin and end with flour mixture, being sure to mix well after each addition. Stir in pecans. Drop dough by rounded teaspoonfuls onto lightly greased cookie sheets. Bake at 350°for 8 minutes. After cookies have baked for 8 minutes, remove from oven. Place a marshmallow half, cut side down, on top of each cookie. Bake for 2 additional minutes. Remove to wire racks. Allow to cool completely before spreading with chocolate frosting and topping with pecan halves. Makes 4 dozen cookies.

(cont.)

CHOCOLATE FROSTING:
2 cups powdered sugar, sifted
¼ cup plus 1 tablespoon cocoa
3 tablespoons butter, softened
¼ cup milk

Combine all frosting ingredients. Beat on medium speed until light and fluffy.

Chocolate Almond Tea Cakes

¾ cup margarine or butter, softened
⅓ cup powdered sugar
1 cup flour
½ cup instant cocoa mix
½ cup toasted almonds, diced
Additional powdered sugar

Combine margarine and ⅓ cup powdered sugar. Stir in flour, cocoa mix, and almonds.
(Refrigerate until firm if dough is too soft to shape.) Heat oven to 325°. Shape dough into
1-inch balls and place on ungreased cookie sheets. Bake for about 20 minutes or until set.
Dip tops into powdered sugar while still warm. Let cool and dip again.

Chocolate Cherry Bars

BASE:
1 chocolate fudge cake mix
1 large can cherry pie filling
1 teaspoon almond extract
2 eggs, beaten

Combine all base ingredients in large bowl until well mixed. Grease
9 x 13-inch baking pan. Pour batter into pan and bake at 350° for 25 to 30 minutes.
When cool, add frosting. Serve with whipped topping or ice cream if desired.

FUDGE FROSTING:
1 cup sugar
5 tablespoons butter or margarine
⅓ cup milk
1 cup semisweet chocolate chips

Combine sugar, butter, and milk in saucepan. Boil for 1 minute, stirring constantly. Remove
from heat and stir in chips until smooth. Let thicken a little and pour over cooled bars.

Chocolate Chip Blond Brownies

2 cups brown sugar
⅔ cup butter, melted
2 eggs
2 teaspoons vanilla
1 to 2 cups flour
1 teaspoon baking powder
¼ teaspoon baking soda
¼ teaspoon salt
½ cup nuts, chopped (optional)
Semisweet chocolate chips (optional)

Add brown sugar to melted butter; cool. Add eggs and vanilla to mixture
and blend well. In separate bowl, sift flour, baking powder, baking soda, and salt.
Add gradually to sugar mixture. Stir in chopped nuts if desired.
Pour mixture into greased 8 x 12-inch baking pan. Sprinkle chocolate chips on top if
desired. Bake at 350° for 20 to 25 minutes. (Do not overcook.) Cut into squares.

Chocolate Chip Coconut Cookies

⅓ cup shortening
⅓ cup butter, softened
½ cup sugar
½ cup brown sugar
1 egg
1 teaspoon vanilla
1½ cups flour
½ teaspoon baking soda
½ teaspoon salt
1 cup semisweet chocolate chips
¼ package flaked coconut
1 to 2 cups oats

Mix shortening, butter, sugars, egg, and vanilla. Blend in flour, baking soda, and salt.
Mix in chocolate chips, coconut, and oats. Drop by rounded teaspoonfuls 2 inches apart
onto ungreased baking sheets. Bake at 375° for 8 to 10 minutes.
Cool slightly before removing from baking sheets.

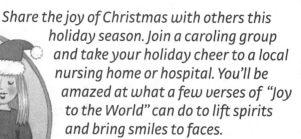

Share the joy of Christmas with others this holiday season. Join a caroling group and take your holiday cheer to a local nursing home or hospital. You'll be amazed at what a few verses of "Joy to the World" can do to lift spirits and bring smiles to faces.

Joy to the world, the Lord is come!
Let earth receive her King;
Let every heart prepare Him room,
And heaven and nature sing,
And heaven and nature sing,
And heaven, and heaven, and nature sing.
—ISAAC WATTS

Chocolate Chip
Cream Cheese Cookies

4 egg yolks
2 cups butter (no substitutions), softened
2 cups sugar
2 (8 ounce) packages cream cheese
2 tablespoons almond extract
4 cups flour
Pinch salt

Combine egg yolks, butter, and sugar. Add cream cheese and almond extract. In separate bowl, combine flour and salt; add to butter mixture. Drop by spoonfuls onto ungreased cookie sheets and bake at 375° until edges turn light brown, approximately 10 minutes.

Chocolate Cookie Bars

CRUST:

1¾ cups flour   ¼ cup cocoa
¾ cup sugar   1 cup butter

In medium bowl, stir together flour, sugar, and cocoa; cut in butter until crumbly (mixture will be dry). Press firmly onto bottom of 9 x 13-inch baking pan. Bake at 350° for 15 minutes.

FILLING:

1 cup semisweet chocolate chips
1 (14 ounce) can sweetened condensed milk
1 teaspoon vanilla

While crust is cooking, combine chocolate chips, condensed milk, and vanilla in medium saucepan. Cook over medium heat, stirring constantly until chips are melted. Pour over baked crust.

(cont.)

TOPPING:
1 cup nuts, chopped
1 cup semisweet chocolate chips

Top crust and filling with nuts and chocolate chips. Bake at 350° for 20 minutes.

Chocolate Holiday Cookies

COOKIES:
⅔ cup powdered sugar
½ cup butter or margarine, softened
½ teaspoon vanilla
1 cup flour
2 tablespoons cocoa
⅛ teaspoon salt

Beat together powdered sugar, butter, and vanilla at medium speed. Reduce speed and add flour, cocoa, and salt. Divide dough in half. One half at a time, place dough between sheets of lightly floured waxed paper and roll out to ⅛-inch thickness, refrigerating remaining half. Remove paper and cut dough with 2- to 2½-inch cookie cutters. Place on ungreased cookie sheets. Bake at 325° for 14 to 18 minutes. Cool cookies completely before decorating with icing as desired.

(cont.)

ICING:
1¼ cups powdered sugar
1 tablespoon meringue powder
2 tablespoons warm water
¼ teaspoon cream of tartar

Combine all icing ingredients and beat at low speed until moistened. Increase speed and beat until stiff and glossy. Add more warm water if icing becomes too stiff. Cover with damp paper towel until ready to use.

Trim a favorite photo to fit inside a holiday cookie-cutter shape. Glue the edges of the picture to the inside of the cutter. You can add ribbon, lace, glitter, and paint to the cutter as desired. Remember to label the picture with name and date. Hang on the tree. Make a collection to show the growth of a child or changes in the family's appearance over the years. This makes a delightful gift for Grandma.

Chocolate Nut Caramel Bars

2 cups semisweet chocolate chips
2 tablespoons vegetable oil
40 caramels, unwrapped
5 tablespoons margarine
2 tablespoons water
1 cup peanuts, chopped

Melt (over hot water) chocolate chips and vegetable oil. Stir until smooth. Pour half
of mixture into 8 x 8-inch baking pan, spreading evenly. Refrigerate until firm.
In saucepan, combine caramels, margarine, and water; heat until smooth.
Add nuts and pour over chocolate mixture. Then reheat other half
of chocolate mixture; pour over caramel layer. Set several hours until firm.

Chocolate Peanut Butter Squares

1 cup butter, melted
2½ cups peanut butter
5 cups powdered sugar
4 tablespoons butter, melted
1 cup semisweet chocolate chips

Mix butter and peanut butter until smooth. Add powdered sugar. Press firmly into 9 x 13-inch baking pan. Over low heat, stir melted butter and chocolate chips until smooth. Spread on top of peanut butter mixture. Refrigerate for 2 hours. Cut into squares.

Chocolate Spritz Cookies

1¼ cups butter, softened
1 cup sugar
⅔ cup dark brown sugar
2 large eggs
1 teaspoon vanilla
½ teaspoon baking soda
¼ teaspoon salt
⅔ cup cocoa
2½ cups flour

Cream butter and sugars until light and fluffy. Add eggs one at a time. Add vanilla. In separate bowl, combine baking soda, salt, cocoa, and flour; add gradually to creamed mixture until just blended. Use cookie press fitted with disk of choice. Press cookies 2 inches apart onto ungreased cookie sheets. Bake at 375° for 10 minutes.

Chocolate-Striped Cookies

½ cup butter, softened
½ cup shortening
1 cup sugar
½ teaspoon baking soda
⅛ teaspoon salt
1 egg
2 tablespoons milk
1 teaspoon vanilla

3 cups flour
⅓ cup semisweet chocolate chips,
  melted and cooled
½ cup nuts, finely chopped
½ cup mini semisweet
  chocolate chips
¼ teaspoon almond extract

Beat butter and shortening on medium to high speed for 30 seconds. Add sugar, baking soda, and salt; beat until combined. Beat in egg, milk, and vanilla. Beat in as much flour as possible with mixer; stir in remaining flour by hand. Divide dough in half. Knead melted chocolate and nuts into half of dough. Knead miniature chocolate pieces and almond extract into other half. Divide each portion of dough in half. Line bottom and sides of 9 x 5 x 3-inch loaf pan with plastic wrap. Press half of chocolate dough evenly in pan. Layer with half of vanilla dough, remaining chocolate dough, then remaining vanilla dough to form four even, flat layers. Invert pan to remove dough and peel off plastic wrap. Cut dough crosswise into ¼-inch-thick slices. Place cookies 2 inches apart on ungreased cookie sheets. Bake at 375° for about 10 minutes.

For a gift that will keep on giving, buy a cookie jar and fill it with your home-baked cookies. You can even include the recipe. Wrap up the jar in gift wrap or a piece of holiday fabric.

Chocolate Syrup Brownies

BROWNIE LAYER:

½ cup butter or margarine, softened
1 cup sugar
4 eggs
1 (16 ounce) bottle chocolate-flavored syrup
1¼ cups flour
1 cup walnuts, chopped

Cream butter and sugar; beat in eggs. Blend in syrup and flour; stir in nuts. Pour into greased 9 x 13-inch baking pan. Bake at 350° for 30 to 35 minutes. Cool slightly before frosting. Cool completely; cut into bars.

QUICK FROSTING:

⅔ cup sugar
3 tablespoons milk
3 tablespoons butter
½ cup semisweet chocolate chips

Mix sugar, milk, and butter; bring to a boil and boil for 30 seconds. Remove from heat; stir in chocolate chips until melted. Frosting will be thin. Spread over brownies.

Chocolate Trio Squares

LAYER 1:

¼ cup butter, softened   ¼ teaspoon salt
1 cup flour, sifted

Cream together above ingredients and spread in greased and floured
9 x 9-inch square baking pan. Bake at 350° for 15 minutes.

LAYER 2:

2 eggs   1 teaspoon vanilla
¼ cup brown sugar   ¼ teaspoon salt
1 cup walnuts, finely chopped 2 tablespoons flour
½ cup flaked coconut

Combine eggs and brown sugar; beat well. Add nuts, coconut, vanilla, salt, and flour.
Mix well. Spread over first baked layer. Bake at 350° for 15 minutes. Cool in pan.

(cont.)

LAYER 3 (ICING):
1 cup semisweet chocolate chips
¼ cup light corn syrup
1 tablespoon water
Walnuts, chopped (optional)

Melt chocolate chips in microwave, then add corn syrup and water.
Spread icing over second layer. Sprinkle with nuts if desired.

Chunky Chocolate Cookies

1 (4 ounce) sweet chocolate bar
½ cup butter
½ cup sugar
¼ cup brown sugar
1 egg
1 teaspoon vanilla
1 cup flour
½ teaspoon baking soda
½ teaspoon salt
½ cup nuts, coarsely chopped

Chop chocolate bar into bite-sized pieces; set aside. Cream butter until soft. Add sugars, egg, and vanilla; beat until light and fluffy. Add flour, baking soda, and salt. Stir in chocolate pieces and nuts. Drop by teaspoonfuls 2 inches apart onto ungreased cookie sheets. Bake at 375° for 8 to 10 minutes or until lightly browned.

Look for joy in the simple things this year. Instead of tiring yourself out while trying to make this Christmas more spectacular than the last, relax and focus on the little things— read the Christmas story with your family, decorate the tree with your kids (don't worry if it doesn't look perfect!), play in the snow, eat one more cookie (don't worry about your diet), and direct your thoughts toward that first Christmas, when the Lord sent the gift of baby Jesus out of His amazing love for us.

Double Chocolate Mud Bars

½ cup butter, softened
1 cup sugar
2 large eggs, separated
1½ cups flour
1 teaspoon baking powder
½ teaspoon salt

1 cup walnuts, chopped
½ cup semisweet chocolate chips
1 cup miniature marshmallows
1 cup candy-coated chocolate pieces
    (optional)
1 cup brown sugar, packed

Beat together butter and sugar. Beat egg yolks one at a time. In separate bowl, mix together flour, baking powder, and salt. Fold flour mixture into butter mixture. Press into greased 9 x 13-inch baking pan. Sprinkle with nuts, chocolate chips, marshmallows, and, if desired, candy-coated chocolate pieces. Beat egg whites at high speed until stiff peaks form. Fold in brown sugar. Spread over mixture in pan. Bake at 350° for 35 minutes. Cool completely; cut into squares.

Fudge-Topped Brownies

BROWNIE LAYER:

1 cup butter, melted
2 cups sugar
1 cup flour
⅔ cup cocoa
½ teaspoon baking powder

2 eggs
½ cup milk
1½ teaspoons vanilla
1 cup nuts, chopped (optional)

In large mixing bowl, combine butter, sugar, flour, cocoa, baking powder, eggs, milk, and vanilla. Beat thoroughly. Stir in nuts if desired. Grease 9 x 13-inch baking pan and spread mixture evenly in pan. Bake at 350° for 40 minutes or until brownies just begin to pull away from sides of pan. When brownies are nearly done, begin to mix icing.

ICING:

2 cups semisweet
chocolate chips

1 (14 ounce) can sweetened
condensed milk
1½ teaspoons vanilla

Over low heat, melt chocolate chips in heavy saucepan with milk and vanilla. Remove from heat. Immediately spread over hot brownies. Cool, chill, and cut into bars.

Oatmeal Chocolate Chip Cookies

2½ cups oats
1 cup butter, softened
1 cup brown sugar
1 cup sugar
2 eggs
1 teaspoon vanilla
2 cups flour

½ teaspoon salt
1 teaspoon baking soda
1 teaspoon baking powder
2 cups chocolate chips
1 (4 ounce) chocolate bar, grated
1½ cups walnuts, chopped

Put oats in blender or food processor; blend to a fine powder, then set aside. Cream butter with sugars until fluffy. Add eggs and vanilla; mix together with blended oats, flour, salt, baking soda, and baking powder. Stir in chocolate chips, chocolate bar, and nuts. Roll into balls and place 2 inches apart on lightly greased cookie sheets. Bake at 375° for 10 minutes.

Oven-Shy Cookies

1 (16 ounce) package marshmallows
2 cups semisweet chocolate chips
¼ cup butter or margarine
3 cups crispy rice cereal
1 (12 ounce) can salted peanuts

In saucepan over low heat, cook and stir marshmallows, chips, and butter until marshmallows are melted and mixture is smooth. Remove from heat. Stir in cereal and peanuts; mix well. Drop by rounded tablespoonfuls onto waxed paper to cool.

Peanut Butter Chocolate Kiss Cookies

½ cup shortening
¾ cup peanut butter
⅓ cup sugar
⅓ cup brown sugar, packed
1 egg
2 tablespoons milk

1 teaspoon vanilla
1⅓ cups flour
1 teaspoon baking soda
½ teaspoon salt
Additional sugar
1 package chocolate kisses

Cream shortening and peanut butter. Add sugar and brown sugar. Add egg, milk, and vanilla. Beat well. In large bowl, combine flour, baking soda, and salt. Gradually add creamed mixture and blend thoroughly. Shape dough into 1-inch balls; roll in sugar. Place on ungreased cookie sheets. Bake at 375° for 10 to 12 minutes. Remove from oven immediately and place unwrapped kiss on top of each cookie. Remove from cookie sheets and cool.

Snowcap Brownies

½ cup flour
½ teaspoon salt
½ cup butter or margarine, softened
1 cup sugar
2 eggs
1 teaspoon vanilla
2 (1 ounce) squares unsweetened chocolate, melted
1 cup quick rolled oats
½ cup walnuts, chopped
Powdered sugar

Mix flour and salt; add butter, sugar, eggs, vanilla, and chocolate. Beat until smooth, about 2 minutes. Add rolled oats and walnuts. Spread in greased 8 x 8-inch pan. Bake at 350° for 25 minutes. Cool in pan. Cut into squares and sprinkle with powdered sugar. Makes 16 squares.

Snowmen Cookies

White chocolate almond bark
Nutter Butter sandwich cookies
Mini semisweet chocolate chips

Melt almond bark and spread chocolate on cookies.
Place 2 mini chocolate chips side by side to make eyes.

When preparing cookies to mail, use plastic wrap to package cookies in pairs, back to back.

Thin Chocolate Chip Cookies

1½ cups sugar
1 cup margarine
2 eggs
2 teaspoons vanilla
2½ cups Grape-Nuts Flakes cereal
1 cup semisweet chocolate chips
2 cups flour
1 teaspoon baking soda
⅛ teaspoon salt

Cream sugar and margarine. Add eggs and stir; add vanilla and stir; add cereal and chocolate chips and stir. In separate bowl, combine flour, baking soda, and salt then add gradually to cereal mixture. Stir well. Drop by teaspoonfuls onto ungreased cookie sheets and bake at 350° for 20 minutes or until golden brown. (Bake for a less amount of time for smaller cookies.)

Traditional No-Bake Cookies

½ cup butter or margarine
½ cup milk
2 cups sugar
½ cup cocoa
1 cup peanut butter
1 teaspoon vanilla
3 cups oats

Combine butter, milk, sugar, and cocoa in large saucepan. Bring to a rolling boil.
Boil for 3 minutes (do not overboil) and add peanut butter, vanilla, and oats.
Drop by heaping teaspoonfuls onto sheets of waxed paper. Let cool until firm.
Store in airtight container in cool, dry place.

Triple Chocolate Chip Cookies

1 chocolate cake mix
1 cup sour cream
1 (4 serving size) instant chocolate pudding
1 cup semisweet chocolate chips
2 large eggs

Combine all five ingredients in bowl. Stir until moistened and no large lumps remain.
Drop by rounded spoonfuls about 2 inches apart onto greased cookie sheets.
Bake at 350° for 16 to 18 minutes. Let stand for 2 minutes. Cool completely.

White Chocolate Squares

2 cups white chocolate chips, divided
¼ cup butter or margarine
1 cup flour
½ teaspoon baking powder
1 (14 ounce) can sweetened condensed milk
1 cup pecans or walnuts, chopped
1 large egg
1 teaspoon vanilla
Powdered sugar

Preheat oven to 350°. Grease 9 x 13-inch baking pan. In large saucepan over low heat, melt 1 cup chips and butter. Stir in flour and baking powder until blended. Stir in sweetened condensed milk, nuts, egg, vanilla, and remaining chips. Spoon mixture into prepared pan. Bake for 20 to 25 minutes. Cool. Sprinkle with powdered sugar; cut into squares. Store covered at room temperature.

Merry
Desserts

Somehow, not only for Christmas,
But all the long year through,
The joy that you give to others,
Is the joy that comes back to you.
JOHN GREENLEAF WHITTIER

Black Forest Trifle

1 chocolate fudge cake mix
1 (5.9 ounce) package chocolate instant pudding
1 quart cherry pie filling
3 cups whipping cream, whipped
Chocolate curls
Maraschino cherries

Prepare cake mix according to package directions and bake in two layers; slice layers into chunks after cake cools. Prepare chocolate pudding according to package directions. In large bowl, layer chunks of chocolate cake, pudding, pie filling, and whipped cream—making three repetitions and ending with layer of cake and cream. Garnish with whipped cream, chocolate curls, and cherries. Chill and serve.

Chocolate Cherry Delicious

2 cans cherry pie filling
1 chocolate cake mix
¾ cup butter, melted

Preheat oven to 350˚. Spread pie filling into 9 x 13-inch baking pan. Sprinkle dry cake mix evenly over filling, then drizzle melted butter over cake mix. (Butter may leave some dry spots on the dessert.) Bake for 45 minutes or until done. Serve warm or cold.

Chocolate Chip Cheeseball

1 (8 ounce) package cream cheese, softened
½ cup butter, softened
¾ cup powdered sugar
2 tablespoons brown sugar
¼ teaspoon vanilla
¾ cup mini semisweet chocolate chips
¾ cup pecans, finely chopped

In medium bowl, combine cream cheese and butter. Beat with hand mixer on low speed until smooth. Stir in powdered sugar, brown sugar, and vanilla. Add chocolate chips; stir. Cover and refrigerate for 2 hours. Form chilled mixture into ball. Wrap in plastic wrap and refrigerate for 1 hour longer. Roll ball in chopped pecans. Keep refrigerated until ready to serve with pretzels or graham crackers.

Chocolate Chip Pumpkin Bread

3 cups powdered sugar
1 (15 ounce) can pumpkin puree
1 cup vegetable oil
⅔ cup water
4 eggs
3½ cups flour
1 tablespoon ground cinnamon

1 tablespoon ground nutmeg
2 teaspoons baking soda
1½ teaspoons salt
1 cup mini semisweet chocolate chips
½ cup walnuts, chopped (optional)

Preheat oven to 350°. Grease and flour three 1-pound size coffee cans or three 9 x 5-inch loaf pans. In large bowl, combine sugar, pumpkin, oil, water, and eggs. Beat until smooth. Blend in flour, cinnamon, nutmeg, baking soda, and salt. Fold in chocolate chips and, if desired, nuts. Fill cans or loaf pans one-half to three-fourths full. Bake for 1 hour or until toothpick inserted in center comes out clean. Cool on wire racks before removing from cans or loaf pans.

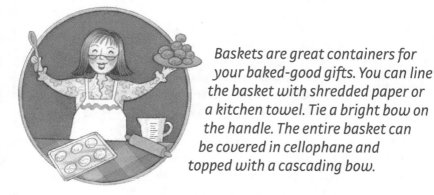

Baskets are great containers for your baked-good gifts. You can line the basket with shredded paper or a kitchen towel. Tie a bright bow on the handle. The entire basket can be covered in cellophane and topped with a cascading bow.

Chocolate Coffee Dessert

Graham cracker squares (not crumbs)
2 cups (1 pint) whipping cream
½ cup powdered sugar
4 tablespoons chocolate syrup
1 tablespoon instant coffee granules
Chocolate garnish (chocolate shavings or chocolate sprinkles)

Place layer of graham crackers in 9 x 9-inch baking pan. Whip cream; add powdered sugar, chocolate syrup, and coffee. Place one-third of mixture on crackers. Repeat with another layer of crackers and second one-third of mixture; top with third layer of crackers and last one-third of mixture. Garnish with chocolate.

Chocolate Delight

1 (4 serving size) package chocolate instant pudding
2 cups milk
2 cups frozen whipped topping, thawed, divided
Garnish (chocolate chips, grated chocolate, chocolate cookie crumbs, or strawberries)

Prepare pudding with milk as directed on package. Fold 1½ cups whipped topping into pudding; spoon into four dessert dishes. Top with remaining ½ cup whipped topping and chocolate or strawberry garnish.

Chocolate Rainbow Rolls

½ cup butter or margarine
2 cups semisweet chocolate chips
6 cups (10½ ounces) miniature colored marshmallows
1 cup nuts, finely chopped
Additional chopped nuts

In medium saucepan over low heat, melt butter and chocolate chips until blended, stirring constantly. Remove from heat and cool for 5 minutes. Stir in marshmallows and 1 cup nuts. (Do not let marshmallows melt.) On sheet of waxed paper, shape mixture into two 7-inch rolls. Wrap rolls in aluminum foil and refrigerate for about 20 to 25 minutes. To coat rolls, roll them in additional nuts. Wrap and refrigerate overnight. Cut rolls into ¼-inch slices. Store in airtight container in a cool, dry place.

Mix up these recipes a bit. Try using some white chocolate or add in some extra ingredients of your own. If it sounds good, try it! You may just discover a new holiday treat that your family will love.

Chocolate Strawberry Mousse

CHOCOLATE BASE:

½ cup shortening
3 (1 ounce) squares unsweetened
   chocolate
1¼ cups sugar
1 teaspoon vanilla

3 eggs
⅔ cup flour
½ teaspoon baking powder
¼ teaspoon salt

Melt shortening and chocolate in saucepan over low heat, stirring until smooth. Remove from heat. Add sugar, vanilla, and eggs. Mix well. In separate bowl, combine flour, baking powder, and salt. Add to chocolate mixture and stir until well blended. Spread into greased 9-inch springform pan. Bake at 350° for 25 to 30 minutes.

TOPPING:

1 package frozen sliced
   strawberries with syrup
1 envelope gelatin, unflavored
½ cup sugar

2 tablespoons lemon juice
2 cups whipping cream, divided
Fresh strawberries (optional)

(cont.)

Drain strawberries and reserve liquid. Add water to make 1¼ cups of liquid. Combine gelatin and sugar in saucepan. Stir in strawberry liquid and lemon juice. Bring to a boil. Stir constantly to dissolve sugar and gelatin. Remove from heat and chill until starting to set. Beat 1¼ cups whipping cream until stiff peaks form. Beat gelatin mix with mixer until light. Fold into whipped cream. Fold in drained strawberries. Spread evenly over base in pan and chill until set, approximately 1½ hours or overnight. To serve, beat remaining whipping cream until stiff peaks form; spread over mousse and garnish with fresh strawberries if desired.

Cranberry Chocolate Orange Rounds

2 cups fresh or frozen cranberries, chopped
½ cup sugar
3½ cups flour
1½ cups sugar
1 teaspoon baking powder
1 teaspoon baking soda
1 teaspoon salt
2 eggs
1½ cups orange juice
¼ cup oil
1 tablespoon orange zest
2 cups semisweet chocolate chips
1 cup nuts, chopped

Combine cranberries and ½ cup sugar and set aside. In separate bowl, combine flour, 1½ cups sugar, baking powder, baking soda, and salt. Beat together eggs, juice, oil, and zest; add to dry ingredients, then stir just until moistened. Fold in cranberry mixture, chocolate chips, and nuts. Divide batter into eight or nine well-greased 10-ounce soup tins. Fill just over half full and bake at 350° for 35 to 40 minutes or until done. Cool for 10 minutes, then run blade of thin knife around edges of tins to loosen. Turn out on wire rack to cool completely. Wrap and store overnight before slicing, or freeze for later use.

Hot Fudge Pudding

1 cup flour
¼ teaspoon salt
2 tablespoons cocoa
2 teaspoons baking powder
¾ cup sugar
½ cup milk
2 tablespoons shortening
1 cup nuts, chopped
4 tablespoons brown sugar
2 tablespoons cocoa
2 cups hot water

Preheat oven to 350°. Mix flour, salt, cocoa, baking powder, and sugar in bowl. Stir in milk, shortening, and nuts. Spread into 9 x 9-inch baking pan. Mix brown sugar and 2 tablespoons cocoa and sprinkle over mixture. Pour hot water over top and bake for 40 minutes. Serve with ice cream or whipped topping.

S'More Pudding Dessert

9 full-size graham crackers, crushed
3¼ cups milk
1 (5 ounce) package (not instant) vanilla pudding
4 (1¼ ounce) chocolate candy bars
2 cups miniature marshmallows

Line bottom of 1½-quart baking dish with one-third of graham cracker crumbs.
Using milk, cook pudding as directed on package; allow to cool for 5 minutes.
Spread half of pudding over graham cracker crumbs, then add another third of
cracker crumbs. Place candy bars next, then spread remaining pudding over
chocolate bars. Finish off layers with remaining third of cracker crumbs;
sprinkle with marshmallows. Broil until golden brown. Serve warm or chilled.

Dear Heavenly Father, thank You for giving me joy. When the winter blues leave me feeling a little less than cheerful, all I need to do is look to You. In an instant, my spirit is lifted and the stress of the holiday diminishes. I praise You, Lord.

Rejoice in the Lord always.
PHILIPPIANS 4:4

Index

JOLLY BEVERAGES

FESTIVE CAKES & PIES

CHRISTMASSY
CANDIES

HOLIDAY COOKIES & BARS

MERRY DESSERTS

Also Available from Mary & Martha. . .

 *In the Kitchen with Mary & Martha*
ISBN 1-59310-878-8

 *One-Dish Wonders*
ISBN 1-59789-011-1

 *Cookin' Up Christmas*
ISBN 1-59789-239-4

224 pages • hardback with printed comb binding

Available Wherever Books Are Sold